Elegantly Simple Vegan Oil-Free Recipes

Vaishnavi • Ananth Kendapadi

Published in the United States of America by
CreateSpace, 2017

Photography by Vaishnavi Vijay

Book layout by Wordplay
www.wordplaynow.com

ISBN: 978-1543225105

To healthy eaters everywhere

V.V, & A.K.

Introduction

During the summer of 2015, my wife and my son were away for almost two months visiting family in India. Though I enjoyed dining at various restaurants, I decided to experiment with cooking and expand my options. I visited the local library, and browsed several books. Almost all of them had a lengthy list of ingredients, and a lengthier description of the steps. I am from an engineering background and I like minimalistic designs and processes. It appeared to me that if the cooking process was described like an engineering process, with a focus on minimalism and efficiency, it may be useful to many. The idea stayed dormant in my mind, I did not take any action. The summer ended, and my family came back.

A few months later, in December 2015, my sister-in-law, Vaishnavi, and her family visited us. During the course of conversation, I shared my views on a cookbook that was focused on minimalism and efficiency. The very next day, she documented one of her family recipes in the very format that I had in my mind. It was very impressive and I asked her if she would be interested in partnering with me to capture a number of other recipes in the same format. Since both of us believe in plant-based food, we decided to use only plant-based recipes. She began working with several recipes from her friends and family, adding and removing ingredients. By continuous experimentation, she came up with a list of about 50 recipes, each with minimal set of ingredients. After a month, we decided to extend the idea further, and decided to make our recipes oil-free as well.

Most of the recipes here are well known to many families across the globe. Our only innovation is to keep the list of ingredients and the steps for each really minimal by removing all the non-essentials and to capture the process visually on a single page.

We hope that you find this book useful, and that it helps you in your goal to eat healthily and feel your best, even on your busiest days.

Ananth

Contents

Soups

Carrot Ginger Soup

Ingredients: carrots, vegetable broth, onions, ginger, red chili powder, salt

Time: ~25 minutes

1 Finely chop two medium-sized carrots.	2 Heat one and ½ cups of vegetable broth in a pan.	3 Stir in the carrots.
4 Finely chop one medium-sized onion. Add it to the mix.	5 Add one teaspoon of finely chopped ginger.	6 Boil until the carrots turn soft.
7 Turn off heat. Add one teaspoon each of red chili powder and salt.	8 Add ½ cup water. Pour the mixture in a blender and puree until smooth.	Transfer to a bowl and serve.

Cauliflower Soup

Ingredients: cauliflower, vegetable broth, onions, salt, black pepper

Optional: fresh herbs of your choice

Time: ~30 minutes

1 Wash one head of cauliflower and chop into florets.	2 Get three cups of vegetable broth ready.	3 Chop one onion, heat a nonstick pan to medium temperature, and put the onion in the pan.
4 Add two teaspoons of salt and cook until the onion becomes soft.	5 Add the vegetable broth.	6 Add the cauliflower florets and bring to a boil.
7 Cover and cook until the cauliflower turns soft. Turn off heat.	8 Let soup cool. Add one teaspoon of black pepper.	9 Transfer to a bowl and serve. If you like, garnish with a fresh herb of your choice.

Kale Potato Soup

Ingredients: baby kale, potatoes, vegetable broth, salt, black pepper

Time: ~30 minutes

1 Prepare one cup of chopped baby kale.	2 Wash three potatoes. Peel and chop them finely.	3 Heat two cups of water in a pan or a pot.
4 Add two cups of vegetable broth.	5 Add the potatoes and bring to a boil.	6 Cover and boil for 10 minutes or until the mix turns soft.
7 Add kale leaves and heat for 10 minutes. Turn off heat.	8 Add one teaspoon each of salt and black pepper.	9 Mix the contents well. Transfer to a bowl and serve.

Mixed Vegetable Soup

Ingredients: tomatoes, mixed vegetables, vegetable broth, salt, black pepper

Time: ~30 minutes

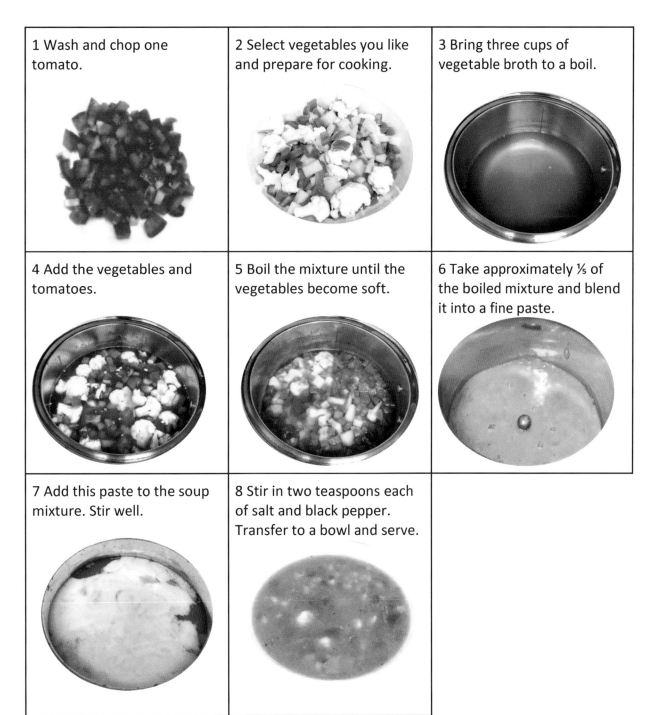

1 Wash and chop one tomato.	2 Select vegetables you like and prepare for cooking.	3 Bring three cups of vegetable broth to a boil.
4 Add the vegetables and tomatoes.	5 Boil the mixture until the vegetables become soft.	6 Take approximately ⅛ of the boiled mixture and blend it into a fine paste.
7 Add this paste to the soup mixture. Stir well.	8 Stir in two teaspoons each of salt and black pepper. Transfer to a bowl and serve.	

Pasta Lentil Soup

Ingredients: vegetable broth, lentils, tomatoes, pasta, garlic powder, salt

Time: ~40 minutes

1 Heat three cups of vegetable broth in a pot. 	2 Add one cup of washed, uncooked lentils of your choice. 	3 Chop one tomato and add to the mix. Bring to a boil. 
4 Add one teaspoon of garlic powder and two teaspoons of salt. 	5 Boil until the lentils turn soft, 25-30 minutes. 	6 Meanwhile, in a separate pan, heat enough water to cook pasta. 
7 Bring water to a boil, then add pasta of your choice and let boil for 10 minutes. 	8 Turn off the heat and drain the pasta. 	9 Stir lentil mixture and pasta together well. Transfer to a bowl and serve. 

Potato Mushroom Soup

Ingredients: red potatoes, mushrooms, garlic, tomatoes, vegetable stock, salt, black pepper

Time: ~30 minutes

1 Wash and chop three red potatoes. 	2 Measure one to two cups of sliced mushrooms. 	3 Finely chop two cloves of garlic. Heat one teaspoon of water in a pan, and then add garlic. 
4 Chop one tomato. When garlic is soft, add tomatoes and cook until soft. 	5 Add the mushrooms. Cover and heat for five minutes. 	6 Add potatoes and two cups of vegetable stock. 
7 Boil until the vegetables turn soft. 	8 Add one teaspoon each salt and black pepper and mix well. 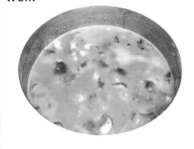	9 Transfer to a bowl and serve. 

Starters and Side Dishes

Baked Sweet Potato Fries

Ingredients: sweet potatoes, red chili powder, turmeric powder, lime, salt

Optional: basil

Preparation time: ~10 minutes

Baking time: ~20 minutes

1 Preheat oven to 425 F. Peel two sweet potatoes. 	2 Slice the sweet potatoes, then cut into thin strips. 	3 Mix together one teaspoon each of red chili powder, salt, and turmeric power. Sprinkle the spice mix on the potatoes. 
4 Sprinkle the juice from one lime evenly over the potatoes. 	5 Arrange the fries on a baking sheet in a single layer and bake for 20 minutes. 	6 Let cool slightly, then transfer to a plate and serve. Garnish with basil if you like. 

Broccoli Crisps

Ingredients: broccoli, gram flour (also known as besan or garbanzo bean flour), red chili powder, salt, black pepper

Preparation time: ~8 minutes

Baking time: ~20 mi

1 Preheat oven to 440 F. Rinse and drain the florets of one head of broccoli. 	2 In a bowl, measure ½ cup of gram flour. 	3 Add one teaspoon of red chili powder, and salt and black pepper if desired. 
4 Add ½ cup water and mix well. 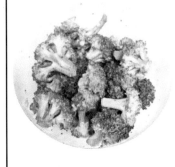	5 Add the broccoli florets and toss evenly to coat. 	6 Spread the broccoli on a baking tray and place it in the oven. 
7 Bake for 20 minutes. 	8 Transfer to plate and enjoy with your favorite dip.	

Chickpea Popcorn

Ingredients: chickpeas, ground cumin, red chili powder, garlic salt

Preparation time: ~6 minutes

Baking time: ~25 minutes

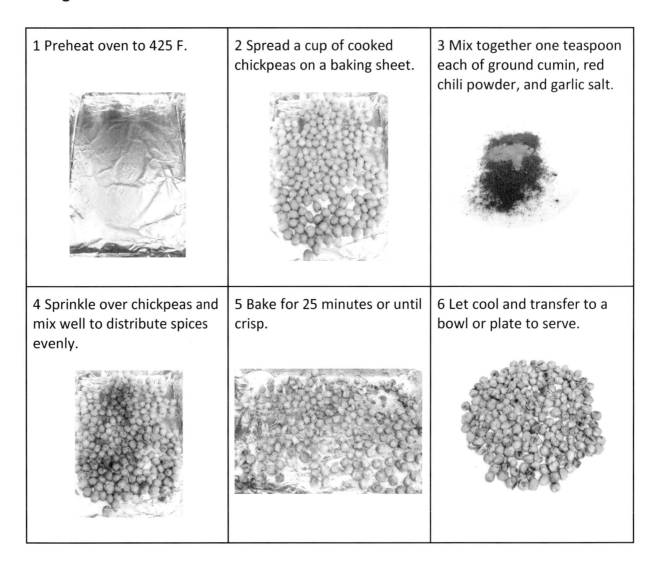

1 Preheat oven to 425 F.	2 Spread a cup of cooked chickpeas on a baking sheet.	3 Mix together one teaspoon each of ground cumin, red chili powder, and garlic salt.
4 Sprinkle over chickpeas and mix well to distribute spices evenly.	5 Bake for 25 minutes or until crisp.	6 Let cool and transfer to a bowl or plate to serve.

Garlic Beet Chips

Ingredients: beets, garlic powder, salt, black pepper

Preparation time: ~10 minutes

Baking time: ~10 minutes

1 Preheat oven to 350 F. Wash and peel one beet.	2 Cut the beet into slices, as thin as possible.	3 Mix one teaspoon each of garlic powder, salt, and black pepper together in a shallow bowl.
4 Add beet slices and toss to coat evenly.	5 Arrange the beets on a baking sheet in a single layer and bake for 10 minutes.	6 Let cool slightly, then transfer to a plate and serve.

Garlic Tofu Crisps

Ingredients: tofu, ground almonds, garlic powder, red chili powder, salt, black pepper

Time: ~30 minutes

1 Preheat the oven to 440 F. Open a 14-ounce package of tofu and drain water.	2 Pat tofu with tissue paper or a paper towel to dry.	3 Measure two teaspoons of ground almonds into a bowl.
4 Add two teaspoons garlic powder.	5 Add one teaspoon each salt, black pepper, and red chili powder.	6 Mix well, then stir in the drained tofu and toss to get an even coating.
7 Spread the mix on a baking tray in a single layer and place in the oven.	8 Bake for 20 minutes.	9 Transfer to a bowl and serve.

Guacamole

Ingredients: avocados, lime, tomatoes, garlic, onion

Time: ~15 minutes

1 Cut two avocados in half and remove the pits.	2 Scoop the inner flesh into a bowl and mash well.	3 Squeeze half a lime over the avocado and mix well.
4 Add ½ cup chopped tomatoes.	5 Add two finely chopped garlic cloves.	6 Add ½ cup finely chopped onion.
7 Mix together and serve.		

Instant Hummus

Ingredients: chickpeas, garlic, sesame seeds, lime, vegetable broth, salt

Optional: paprika

Time: ~10 minutes

1 Measure one cup cooked chickpeas into a bowl. 	2 Add two whole garlic cloves. 	3 Add two teaspoons sesame seeds. 
4 Squeeze in the juice of one lime and add one teaspoon of salt. 	5 Add two teaspoons vegetable broth and mix well. 	6 Transfer to a blender and blend until smooth. 
7 Transfer to bowl to serve. If you like, sprinkle with paprika. 		

Lentil Cucumber Salad

Ingredients: vegetable broth, lentils, cucumber, carrots, lime, salt

Time: ~35 minutes

1 Bring three cups of vegetable broth to a boil. 	2 Add one cup washed, uncooked lentils of any type. 	3 Cover and cook until the lentils are soft, about 25-30 minutes. 
4 Meanwhile, measure ½ cup grated carrots in a bowl. 	5 Add ½ cup finely chopped cucumber. 	6 Add the cooked lentils. 
Stir in one teaspoon of salt and the juice of half a lime. 	8 Mix well together, transfer to a bowl, and serve. 	

Quick Chickpea Salad

Ingredients: chickpeas, onion, tomato, cucumber, salt

Time: ~10 minutes

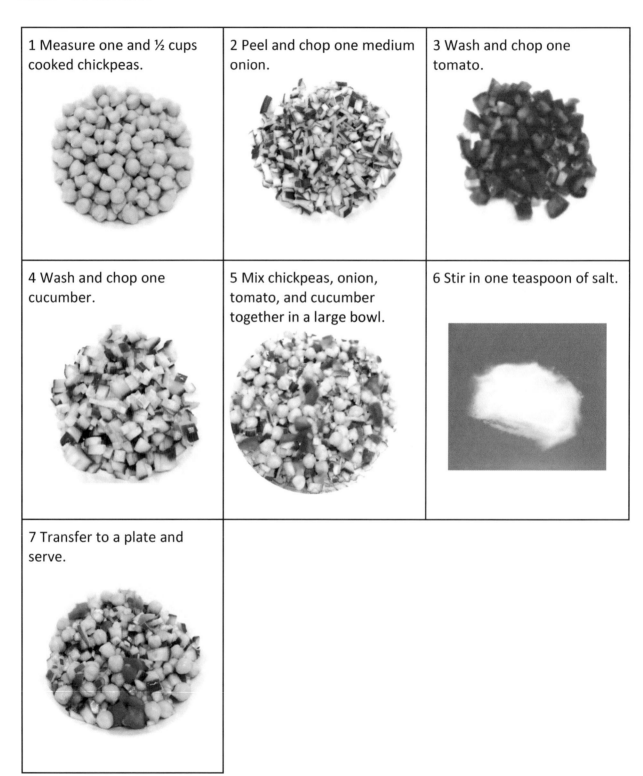

1 Measure one and ½ cups cooked chickpeas.	2 Peel and chop one medium onion.	3 Wash and chop one tomato.
4 Wash and chop one cucumber.	5 Mix chickpeas, onion, tomato, and cucumber together in a large bowl.	6 Stir in one teaspoon of salt.
7 Transfer to a plate and serve.		

Sweet Potato Flatbread

Ingredients: sweet potato, all-purpose flour or whole wheat flour
Preparation time: ~20 minutes
Baking time: ~10 minutes

1 Heat two cups of water in the bottom of a double boiler or pot that accommodates a steamer. 	2 Cut one sweet potato into four pieces, and place in steamer. Cover and steam until the potatoes are soft. 	3 Peel the potatoes, then mash with a fork. Place one cup of the mashed potato in a bowl. 
4 Add one cup of all-purpose or wheat flour to the mashed potatoes, and mix well to get a smooth dough. 	5 Make small balls from the dough. 	6 Flatten each ball and dust with flour. 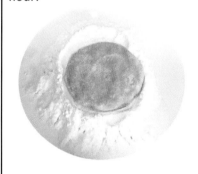
7 Knead balls evenly and pat into desired thickness. 	8 Heat a pan. Cook flatbreads over medium high heat for one minute on each side. 	9 Transfer to a plate and serve. 

Main Dishes

Avocado Brown Rice Noodles

Ingredients: brown rice noodles, avocado, garlic, lemon, salt

Optional: black pepper

Time: ~20 minutes

1 Bring a half pot of water to a boil, and add one teaspoon of salt.	2 Add one package of brown rice noodles.	3 Boil the noodles in water until tender, following instructions on package.
4 Drain the noodles well and transfer to a plate.	5 Meanwhile, place the flesh of one avocado, three cloves of garlic, one teaspoon of lemon juice, and one teaspoon of salt in a bowl or food processor.	6 Blend together until the mixture turns smooth.
7 Top the drained noodles with the avocado mixture.	8 Mix together well.	9 Sprinkle with black pepper if you like, and serve.

Baked Green Beans and Potatoes

Ingredients: green beans, potatoes, lime, garlic powder, salt, black pepper
Preparation time: ~10 minutes
Baking time: ~25 minutes

1 Preheat oven to 425 F. Measure one cup chopped green beans. 	2 Peel two potatoes and finely chop them. 	3 Mix beans and potatoes together. Stir in one teaspoon each salt and black pepper. 
4 Squeeze the juice of half a lime over the beans and potatoes and mix well. 	5 Arrange on a baking sheet in a single layer and bake for 25 minutes. 	6 Transfer to a bowl, sprinkle with one teaspoon of garlic powder, and serve. 

Broccoli Cilantro Pesto with Pasta

Ingredients: broccoli, pasta, cilantro, garlic, lime, salt

Optional: chili flakes

Time: ~30 min

1 Heat two cups of water in the bottom of a double boiler or a pot that accommodates a steamer. 	2 Wash the florets from one head of broccoli. Place over the boiling water, cover, and steam. 	3 Place one cup of water in a separate pan. Add one teaspoon of salt and bring to a boil. 
4 Add desired amount of pasta and cook, following the directions on the package. 	5 Turn off the burner and drain the pasta. 	6 Chop two cups of cilantro, and puree in a blender or food processor. 
7 Add two cloves of garlic to the broccoli, squeeze in the juice of one lime, and add to the cilantro. Puree until smooth. 	8 Mix the pesto with pasta and transfer to plate. 	9 If you like, sprinkle on chili flakes before serving. 

Chia Coconut Oatmeal

Ingredients: rolled oats, chia seeds, coconut, cinnamon

Optional: fruit toppings

Time: ~30 min

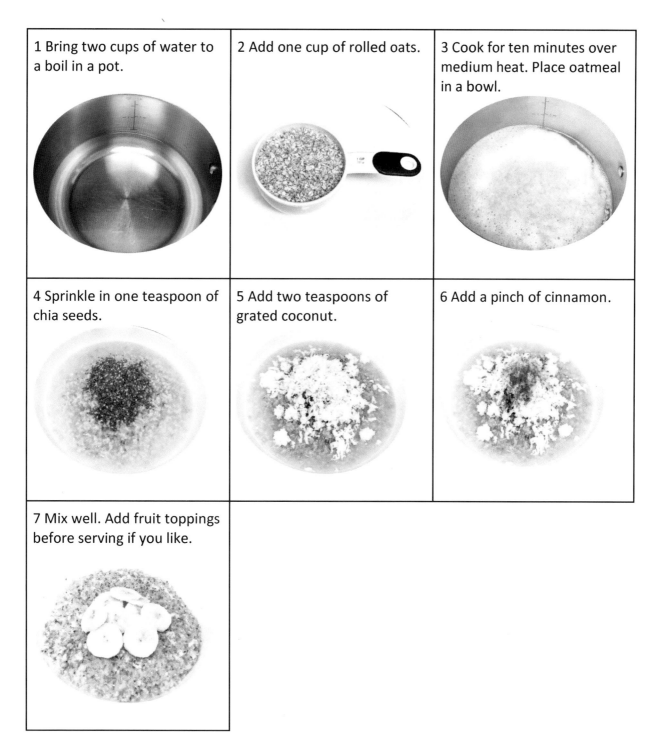

1 Bring two cups of water to a boil in a pot.

2 Add one cup of rolled oats.

3 Cook for ten minutes over medium heat. Place oatmeal in a bowl.

4 Sprinkle in one teaspoon of chia seeds.

5 Add two teaspoons of grated coconut.

6 Add a pinch of cinnamon.

7 Mix well. Add fruit toppings before serving if you like.

Mushroom Curry

Ingredients: onion, mushrooms, cashews, red chili powder, garlic powder, salt

Optional: turmeric, cilantro

Time: ~30 minutes

1 Place one finely chopped onion in a pan over medium heat. 	2 Add two teaspoons of salt and cook until the onions are soft. 	3 Add a bowl of chopped mushrooms. 
4 Heat until mushrooms are cooked, and add another teaspoon of salt. 	5 Blend ⅓ cup of cashews, one teaspoon each of red chili powder and garlic powder, and two teaspoons of water. 	6 Add the cashew mixture to the mushrooms in the pan and mix well. 
7 If you like, add one teaspoon of turmeric power. 	8 Add ½ cup water and heat until mushrooms turn soft. 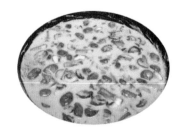	9 Transfer to a bowl. Sprinkle with chopped cilantro before serving if you desire. 

Mushroom Rice

Ingredients: onions, mushrooms, rice, garlic powder, red chili powder, salt

Time: ~30 min

1 Place one finely chopped onion in a pan over medium heat. 	2 Add two teaspoons of salt and cook until the onions are soft. 	3 Add a bowl of chopped mushrooms. 
4 Add two teaspoons of garlic powder and one teaspoon of red chili powder and mix well. 	5 Cover and cook over medium heat for 5 minutes, then add two cups of water and bring to a boil. 	6 Wash and drain one cup of uncooked rice. 
7 Add the rice to the pan, cover, and cook over low heat for 15 minutes. 	8 Turn off the burner, stir once and let sit, covered, for two more minutes. 	9 Transfer to a bowl and serve. 

Pepper Cauliflower

Ingredients: onion, vegetable broth, cumin seed, cauliflower, salt, black pepper

Time: ~25 min

1 Place one finely chopped onion in a pan over medium heat. 	2 Add two teaspoons of salt and cook until the onions are soft. 	3 Stir in two teaspoons of vegetable broth. 
4 Add one teaspoon of cumin seed and two teaspoons of black pepper. 	5 Wash and chop one head of cauliflower. Add to the pan and stir. 	6 Cover and cook over low heat until the cauliflower is soft. 
7 Add more broth if needed. 	8 Transfer to a plate and serve. 	

Quinoa, Beet, and Carrot Mix

Ingredients: beets, carrots, quinoa, lime, salt, black pepper

Time: ~30 min

1 Peel and finely chop one beet and one carrot. 	2 Mix ½ cup quinoa with a cup of water, and bring to a boil. 	3 Reduce heat, cover the mixture and let simmer for about 15 minutes. 
4 While quinoa is cooking, heat two cups of water in a separate pan. 	5 Add the beets and carrots, cover, and cook over medium heat for about 15 minutes. 	6 Turn off heat and drain the beets and carrots. 
7 In a bowl, mix the cooked quinoa with the cooked beets and carrots. 	8 Sprinkle with one teaspoon each of salt and black pepper, and squeeze half a lime over the top. 	9 Mix well and serve. 

Savory Coconut Cabbage

Ingredients: onion, cabbage, ground turmeric, salt, black pepper, grated coconut

Time: ~25 minutes

1 Chop an onion, and heat it in a pan over medium heat.	2 Add two teaspoons salt and sauté.	3 Add one cup water and bring to a boil.
4 While waiting for water to boil, finely chop one small head of white cabbage.	5 Add the cabbage to the onions.	6 Heat for about 10 minutes or until the mixture becomes soft, stirring occasionally.
7 Add one teaspoon each of ground turmeric, salt, and black pepper.	8 Turn off heat and add ½ cup of grated coconut.	9 Mix well, transfer to a bowl, and serve.

Smoothies

Apple Oat Smoothie

Ingredients: apple, rolled oats, cinnamon, almond milk, ice cubes

Time: ~10 minutes

1 Wash and chop one apple.	2 Measure ⅓ cup of rolled oats.	3 Add ½ teaspoon of cinnamon.
4 Measure one cup of almond milk.	5 Combine ingredients in a blender. Add three to six ice cubes and blend until smooth.	6 Pour into a glass and serve.

Blueberry Apple Banana Smoothie

Ingredients: apples, blueberries, banana, almond milk, ice cubes

Time: ~10 minutes

1 Wash and chop two apples.	2 Wash and measure one cup of blueberries.	3 Peel and slice one banana.
4 Measure one cup of almond milk.	5 Combine ingredients in a blender. Add three to six ice cubes and blend until smooth.	6 Pour into a glass and serve.

Blueberry Yogurt Smoothie

Ingredients: vegan yogurt, blueberries, salt, ice cubes

Optional: red chili powder

Time: ~10 minutes

| 1 Measure ⅓ to ½ cup of vegan yogurt. | 2 Add one teaspoon of salt and, if you prefer, a pinch of red chili powder. | 3 Add ½ cup of water and three to six ice cubes. |
| 4 Wash and measure one cup of blueberries. | 5 Combine ingredients in a blender and blend until smooth. | 6 Pour into a glass and serve. |

Ginger Orange Green Smoothie

Ingredients: kale, banana, almond milk, navel orange, ginger, ice cubes

Time: ~10 minutes

1 Wash and chop one cup of fresh kale.	2 Peel and slice one banana.	3 Measure one cup of almond milk.
4 Peel one navel orange and separate into segments.	5 chop one inch of fresh ginger.	6 Put all ingredients in a blender. Add three to six ice cubes and blend until smooth.
7 Pour into a glass and serve.		

Instant Energy Boost Smoothie

Ingredients: apple, banana, orange juice, ice cubes

Time: ~8 minutes

1 Wash and cut one apple.	2 Peel and slice one banana.	3 Measure ¼ cup of orange juice.
4 Put all ingredients in a blender and add three to six ice cubes.	5 Blend until smooth.	6 Pour into a glass and serve.

Mint Cucumber Smoothie

Ingredients: apples, mint leaves, cucumber, ginger, ice cubes

Time: ~10 minutes

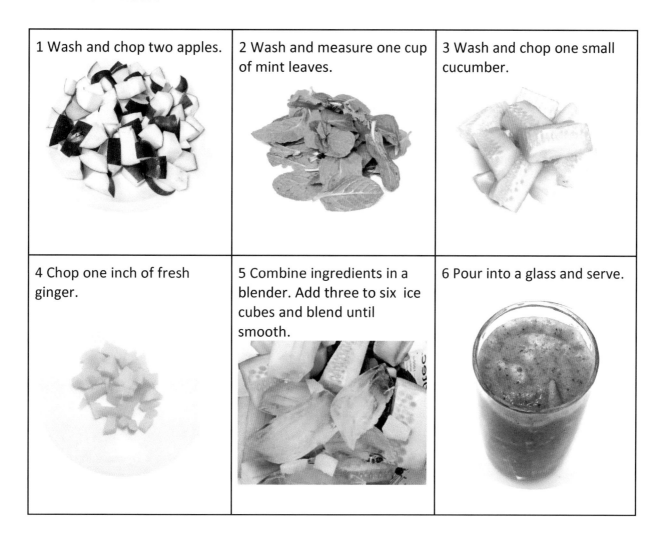

1 Wash and chop two apples.	2 Wash and measure one cup of mint leaves.	3 Wash and chop one small cucumber.
4 Chop one inch of fresh ginger.	5 Combine ingredients in a blender. Add three to six ice cubes and blend until smooth.	6 Pour into a glass and serve.

Papaya Pear Smoothie

Ingredients: papaya, pear, navel orange, almond milk, ice cubes

Time: ~10 minutes

1 Wash, chop, and measure two cups of papaya.	2 Wash, peel, and chop one pear.	3 Peel one navel orange and separate into segments.
4 Measure one cup of almond milk.	5 Put all ingredients in a blender. Add three to six ice cubes and blend until smooth.	6 Pour into a glass and serve.

Protein Boost Smoothie

Ingredients: banana, blueberries, protein powder, almond milk, greens, ice cubes

Time: ~10 minutes

1 Peel and slice one banana.	2 Wash and measure one cup of blueberries.	3 Measure one scoop of protein powder.
4 Measure one cup of almond milk.	5 Measure one cup of fresh greens (kale, spinach, or other of your choice).	6 Combine ingredients in a blender. Add three to six ice cubes and blend until smooth.
7 Pour into a glass and serve.		

Refreshing Kale Smoothie
Ingredients: kale, banana, almond milk, ice cubes
Time: ~7 minutes

1 Wash and chop one cup of fresh kale.	2 Peel and slice one banana.	3 Measure one cup of almond milk.
4 Put all ingredients in a blender and add three to six ice cubes. Blend until smooth.	5 Pour into a glass and serve.	

Spinach Chia Smoothie

Ingredients: banana, spinach, almond milk, chia seeds, ice cubes

Time: ~10 minutes

1 Peel and slice one banana.	2 Measure two cups of fresh baby spinach.	3 Measure cup of almond milk.
4 Place bananas, spinach, and almond milk in a blender and add two teaspoons of chia seeds.	5 Place all ingredients in a blender. Add three to six ice cubes and blend until smooth.	6 Pour into a glass and serve.

Healthy Snacks and Desserts

Almond Date Balls

Ingredients: almonds, pitted dates, peanut butter, cinnamon, salt

Time: ~10 minutes

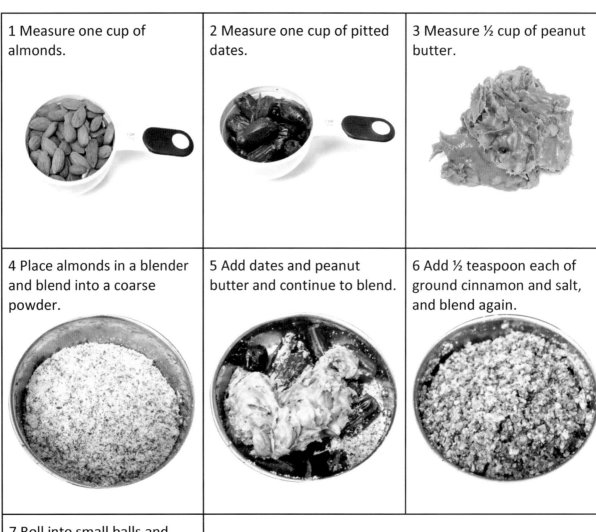

1 Measure one cup of almonds.	2 Measure one cup of pitted dates.	3 Measure ½ cup of peanut butter.
4 Place almonds in a blender and blend into a coarse powder.	5 Add dates and peanut butter and continue to blend.	6 Add ½ teaspoon each of ground cinnamon and salt, and blend again.
7 Roll into small balls and enjoy.		

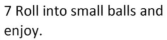

Banana Muffins

Ingredients: bananas, gluten-free baking flour, maple syrup, vanilla almond milk, baking soda

Preparation time: ~10 minutes

Baking time: ~20 to 25 minutes

1 Preheat oven to 350 F. Peel and slice two bananas into a bowl. 	2 Add two cups of gluten-free baking flour. 	3 Add one cup of maple syrup. 
4 Add ½ cup of vanilla almond milk. 	5 Add a pinch of baking soda, and stir until smooth and well-blended. 	6 Place muffin cups on a baking tray, and fill each ¾ full. 
7 Bake for 20 to 25 minutes. 	8 Transfer to a plate and serve. 	

Brownies

Ingredients: gluten-free baking flour, maple syrup, cocoa powder, baking powder, salt, water

Preparation time: ~8 minutes

Baking time: ~20 to 25 minutes

1 Preheat the oven to 350 F. Measure two cups of gluten-free baking flour in a bowl. 	2 Add one cup of maple syrup. 	3 Add ¾ cup of cocoa powder. 
4 Add a pinch each of baking powder and salt. 	5 Add ¾ cup of water and mix well until smooth. 	6 Transfer the mixture to one medium non-stick baking pan or two small ones. 
7 Bake for 20 to 25 minutes. 	8 Let cool. Remove from pan. 	9 Cut into small squares and enjoy. 

Cashew Fudge

Ingredients: cashews, sugar, water

Time: ~20 minutes

1 Measure one cup of cashews and grind into a fine powder in food processor.	2 Heat ½ cup of sugar and ⅓ cup of water in a pan over medium heat.	3 Stir until sugar is completely dissolved.
4 Lower heat, add ground cashews, and mix.	5 Keep stirring until the mixture turns into a soft dough.	6 When mixture has thickened, transfer to a greased surface.
7 Knead and pat until smooth.	8 Cut into squares while warm and let cool.	9 Transfer to a plate and serve.

Chia Cinnamon Pudding

Ingredients: almond milk, maple syrup, chia seeds, cinnamon

Optional: fresh fruit

Time: ~5 minutes, plus overnight refrigeration

1 Measure two cups of almond milk into a bowl.	2 Add two teaspoons of maple syrup.	3 Stir in one tablespoon of chia seeds.
4 Add one teaspoon of cinnamon.	5 Stir well and refrigerate overnight.	6 Add fresh fruit as desired, and enjoy!

Coconut Fudge

Ingredients: sugar, freshly shredded coconut, ground cardamom seed

Time: ~15 minutes

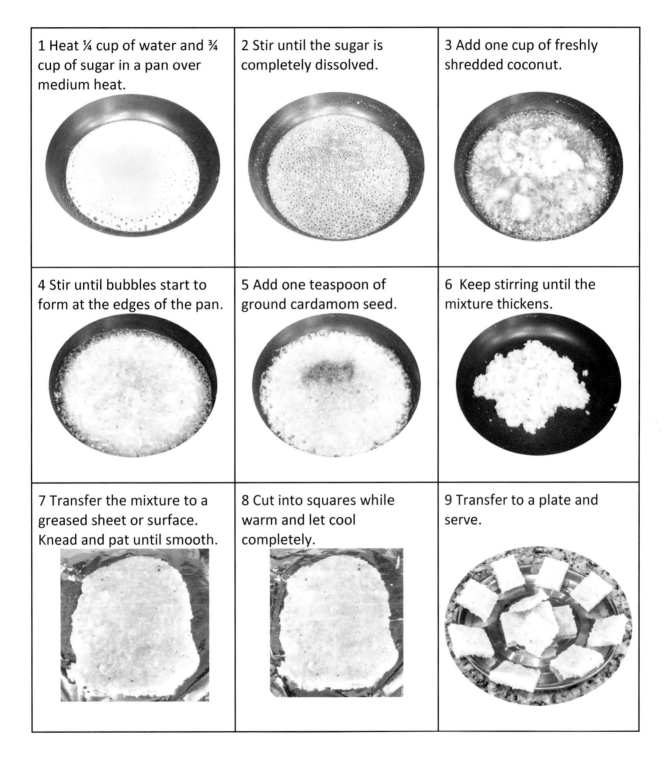

1 Heat ¼ cup of water and ¾ cup of sugar in a pan over medium heat.	2 Stir until the sugar is completely dissolved.	3 Add one cup of freshly shredded coconut.
4 Stir until bubbles start to form at the edges of the pan.	5 Add one teaspoon of ground cardamom seed.	6 Keep stirring until the mixture thickens.
7 Transfer the mixture to a greased sheet or surface. Knead and pat until smooth.	8 Cut into squares while warm and let cool completely.	9 Transfer to a plate and serve.

Granola Bars

Ingredients: rolled oats, almonds, dates, maple syrup, raisins

Time: ~30 minutes, including 10 minutes of baking time and ten minutes of freezer time

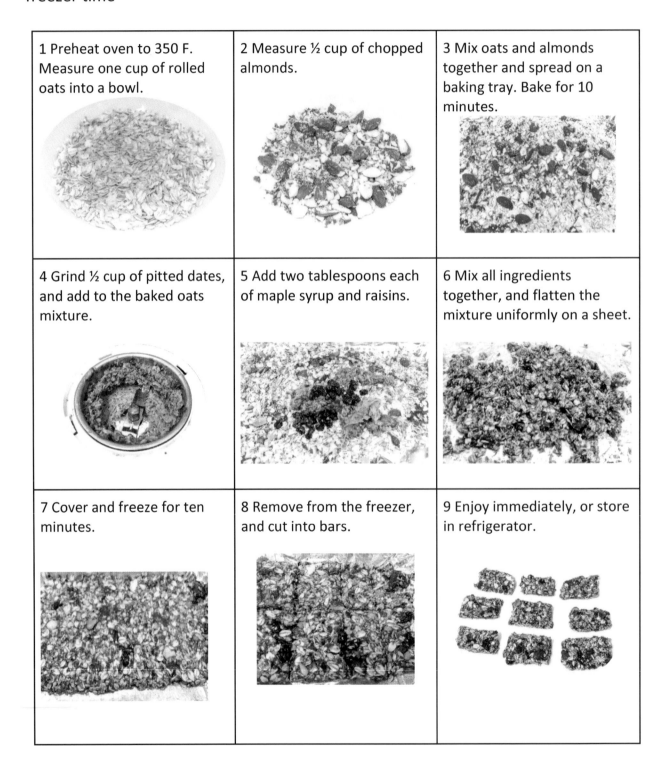

1 Preheat oven to 350 F. Measure one cup of rolled oats into a bowl.	2 Measure ½ cup of chopped almonds.	3 Mix oats and almonds together and spread on a baking tray. Bake for 10 minutes.
4 Grind ½ cup of pitted dates, and add to the baked oats mixture.	5 Add two tablespoons each of maple syrup and raisins.	6 Mix all ingredients together, and flatten the mixture uniformly on a sheet.
7 Cover and freeze for ten minutes.	8 Remove from the freezer, and cut into bars.	9 Enjoy immediately, or store in refrigerator.

Peanut Butter Chickpea Bites

Ingredients: chickpeas, peanut butter, maple syrup, grated coconut

Time: ~10 minutes

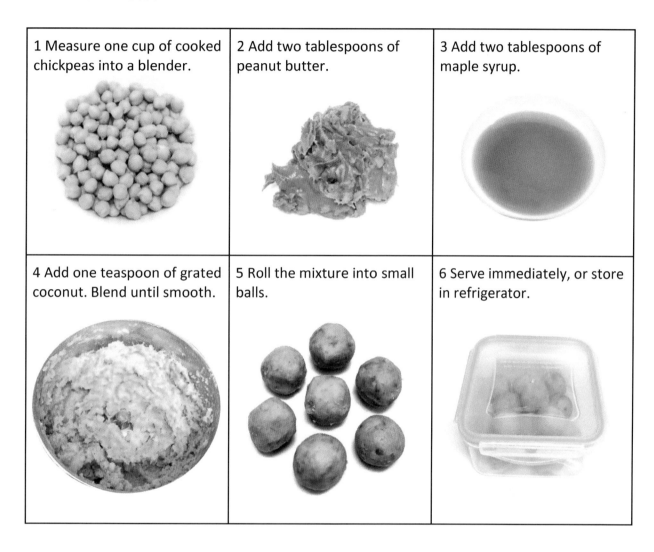

1 Measure one cup of cooked chickpeas into a blender.	2 Add two tablespoons of peanut butter.	3 Add two tablespoons of maple syrup.
4 Add one teaspoon of grated coconut. Blend until smooth.	5 Roll the mixture into small balls.	6 Serve immediately, or store in refrigerator.

Peanut Butter Cookies

Ingredients: unsalted peanut butter, maple syrup, baking soda, salt

Preparation time: ~10 minutes

Baking time: ~10 minutes

1 Preheat oven to 350 F. Measure one cup of unsalted peanut butter into a blender. 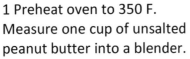	2 Pour in ⅓ cup of maple syrup. 	3 Add a pinch each of baking soda and salt. 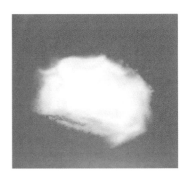
4 Blend the ingredients together. 	5 Use a mini scoop to form balls and drop on a greased baking sheet. 	6 Use a fork to gently flatten them and make a crisscross on each. 
7 Bake for 10 minutes. 	8 Let cookies cool completely before serving. 	

Sticky tamari chicken & togarashi tenderstem

Prep 15 mins | **Cook** 35 mins | **Cals pp** 438 | **Protein** 33g | **Carbs** 37g | **Fat** 17g

We deliver

For the chicken
- 500g free-range chicken thighs
- 25g honey
- 2 tbsp **tamari (soya)**

For the potatoes
- 600g baby white potatoes
- 1 tbsp **sesame oil (sesame)**
- 10g **white sesame seeds (sesame)**

For the broccoli
- 300g tenderstem broccoli
- ½ tsp **shichimi togarashi (sesame)**
- 1 tsp **rice wine vinegar (sulphites)**

To serve
- 2 spring onions
- 10g **white sesame seeds (sesame)**

Allergens in bold
Please wash all fresh produce before use

You cook

1. Preheat the oven to 240C / fan 220C / gas mark 8. Place the **potatoes** on a lined baking tray and drizzle with the **sesame oil**; season with sea salt and black pepper. Roast for 25-30 mins, until becoming golden, turning halfway through.

2. Heat a medium frying pan on a medium heat with 2 tsp oil. Season the **chicken** with sea salt and black pepper, then place in the pan. Cook for 10 mins, turning halfway through.

3. Make the **tamari-honey glaze**; mix the **honey**, **tamari** and 1 tsp oil in a bowl.

4. When the **chicken** has been cooking for 10 mins, pour over the **glaze**. Turn the heat up to high and continue to cook for 5-7 mins, turning regularly, until the **glaze** has reduced and becomes sticky. Check your **chicken** is cooked through by cutting a large piece in half; the flesh should be white and the juices running clear. Cook for longer if necessary, then keep warm in the pan.

5. Meanwhile, bring a large saucepan of lightly salted water to the boil. Five mins before the **potatoes** are ready, place the **broccoli** in the pan and cook on a high heat for 3-4 mins or until cooked but still retaining a slight bite. Drain and add to a bowl with the **shichimi togarashi** and **vinegar**; toss to combine.

6. Thinly slice the **spring onions**. When the **potatoes** are cooked, scatter over **half the sesame seeds** and toss together. Slice the **sticky chicken**.

7. Serve the **chicken** with the **potatoes** and **broccoli**. Garnish with the **spring onions** and **remaining sesame seeds**.

Free-range British chicken

Crispy tofu nuggets
& smoky beans VG

Prep 15 mins I **Cook** 45 mins I **Cals pp** 610 I **Protein** 28g I **Carbs** 89g I **Fat** 16g

We deliver

For the nuggets
- 2 tbsp Mindful Chef Mexican spice mix
- 8 tbsp cornflour
- 600g **firm tofu (soya)**

For the smoky beans
- 1 shallot
- 120g baby plum tomatoes
- 1 tsp smoked paprika
- 200g passata
- 1 tbsp aged **balsamic vinegar (sulphites)**
- 1 tbsp **tamari (soya)**
- 2 tsp cornflour mix (see above)
- 240g cannellini beans (drained)

For the sides
- 900g sweet potatoes
- 180g green beans

Allergens in bold
Dietary symbols | Vegan VG
Please wash all fresh produce before use

You cook

1. Preheat the oven to 220C / fan 200C / gas mark 7. Cut the **potatoes** into **fries** and place on a large, lined baking tray. Drizzle with 1 tsp oil; season with sea salt and black pepper. Mix. Bake for 30 mins, until golden, turning halfway.

2. In a large bowl, combine the **spice mix** and **cornflour**. Remove **2 tsp spiced cornflour** into a smaller bowl and reserve for later. Drain the **tofu** and pat dry with paper towel. Cut each block into 12 cubes, then place in the large bowl of **spiced cornflour**; toss to coat evenly.

3. Heat a large frying pan with 1 tbsp oil on a medium heat. Cook the **tofu** for 3 mins on each side, until turning golden, then transfer to a baking tray. Season well with sea salt and black pepper, then bake for 10-15 mins, until hot and crispy.

4. Boil a kettle. Make the **smoky beans**; finely dice the **shallot** and halve the **tomatoes**. Clean the frying pan and reheat with 1 tsp oil on a medium heat. Add the **shallot** and **paprika**, cook for 3 mins, then add the **passata, tomatoes, vinegar, tamari** and 100ml boiling water. Add 3 tbsp cold water to the **reserved cornflour**, mix to dissolve, then stir into the **smoky sauce**. Drain the **cannellini beans**, rinse, then add to the pan and simmer for 5-10 mins, until thickening.

5. Trim the **green beans**, place in a saucepan and cover with boiling water. Boil for 3-4 mins, then drain.

6. Serve the **tofu nuggets** with the **fries, green beans** and **smoky beans**.

Protein Bars

Ingredients: rolled oats, vegan protein powder, banana, cinnamon

Preparation time: ~9 minutes

Baking time: ~10 minutes

1 Preheat the oven to 350 F. Measure one cup of rolled oats into a bowl. 	2 Add two scoops of vegan protein powder. 	3 Blend oats and protein powder together. 
4 Peel and slice one large banana, and add to the mixture. Add one teaspoon of cinnamon. Stir well. 	5 Spread on a greased sheet. 	6 Cut into bars. 
7 Bake for 10 minutes. 	8 Let cool. Transfer to a plate and enjoy. 	

Protein Brownie Bites

Ingredients: bananas, vegan protein powder, cocoa powder, maple syrup

Preparation time: ~9 minutes

Baking time: ~20 minutes

1 Preheat the oven to 350 F. Peel and slice two ripe bananas into a blender.	2 Add one scoop of vegan protein powder.	3 Add ½ cup of cocoa powder.
4 Add ⅓ cup of maple syrup.	5 Blend well.	6 Arrange non-stick baking cups evenly on a baking tray.
7 Fill each cup ¾ full, and bake for 20 minutes.	8 Let cool before serving.	

Semolina Pudding

Ingredients: semolina, sugar, ground cardamom see

Optional: cashews or almonds for topping

Time: ~15 minutes

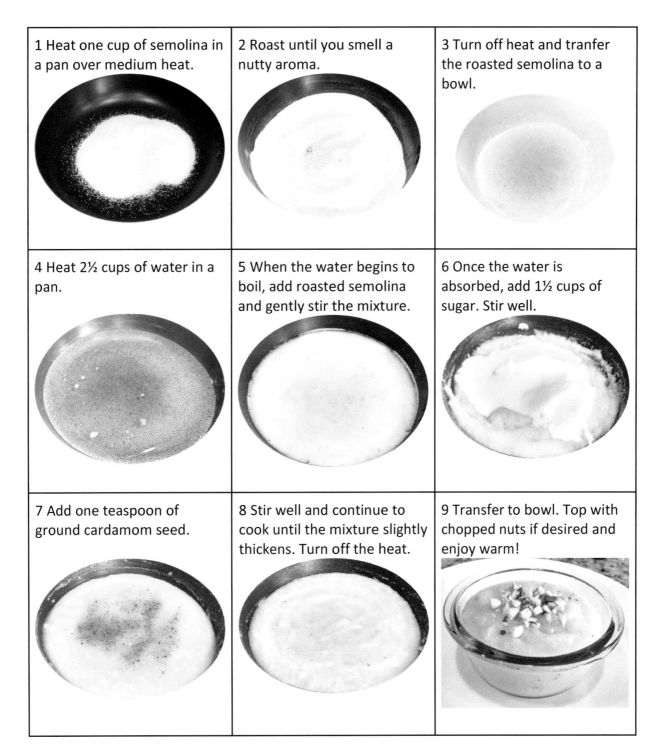

1 Heat one cup of semolina in a pan over medium heat.	2 Roast until you smell a nutty aroma.	3 Turn off heat and tranfer the roasted semolina to a bowl.
4 Heat 2½ cups of water in a pan.	5 When the water begins to boil, add roasted semolina and gently stir the mixture.	6 Once the water is absorbed, add 1½ cups of sugar. Stir well.
7 Add one teaspoon of ground cardamom seed.	8 Stir well and continue to cook until the mixture slightly thickens. Turn off the heat.	9 Transfer to bowl. Top with chopped nuts if desired and enjoy warm!

Sweet Peanut Balls

Ingredients: roasted unsalted peanuts, brown sugar

Time: ~8 minutes

1 Measure one cup of roasted unsalted peanuts into a blender.	2 Add ½ cup of brown sugar.	3 Blend peanuts and brown sugar together until smooth.
4 Transfer to a bowl.	5 Roll mixture into balls and enjoy.	

Printed in Great Britain
by Amazon

62872550R00037